OCT 1 8 2002

W9-BJM-254

DISCARDED

Property of
Nashville Public Library
615 Church St., Nashville, TN 37219

Living in a World of
white
Where Survival Means Blending In

Tanya Lee Stone

BLACKBIRCH PRESS, INC.
WOODBRIDGE, CONNECTICUT

For my sweet Mom, Eileen Cowell.

Published by Blackbirch Press, Inc.
260 Amity Road
Woodbridge, CT 06525

Email: staff@blackbirch.com
Web site: www.blackbirch.com

©2001 by Blackbirch Press, Inc.
First Edition

All rights reserved. No part of this book may be reproduced in any form without permission in writing from Blackbirch Press, Inc., except by a reviewer.

Printed in the United States

10 9 8 7 6 5 4 3 2 1

Photo Credits: All images ©Corel Corporation, except page 6 (right): ©Digital Stock Corp.; pages 7, 14 (inset), 19, 21, 22 (inset): ©www.arttoday.com; pages 12, 18, 20: ©PhotoDisc, Inc.

Library of Congress Cataloging-in-Publication Data
Stone, Tayna Lee.
Living in a world of white / by Tayna Lee Stone.
        p.   cm.
ISBN 1-56711-580-2 (hardcover: alk. paper)
1. Zoology—Polar Regions —Juvenile literature. [1. Zoology—Polar regions. 2. Adaptation (Biology) 3. Animals — Habits and behavior.] I. Title.
QL104.S76   2001
591.7'0911—dc21   2001002353

Contents

What do all of the animals in this book have in common?
They all live in a world of white. They all make their homes in or near the icy,
snowy, frozen habitats of the Arctic and Antarctic. The Arctic is at the North Pole.
Antarctica is at the South Pole. The 10 animals in this book all have special ways
of surviving in these places where there is little food and temperatures
are cold year round. How do they do it?

Did You Know?

- Most wolves dig dens. But during the Arctic winter, the ground can be solid ice. Digging is not possible. Instead, arctic wolves find caves or large cracks in rocks to use as dens.

- Arctic wolves will hunt in an area as large as 1,000 square miles (1,609 square kilometers) to find food.

4

Arctic Wolves

Wintry Wanderers

Arctic wolves live so far north in Canada and Greenland that people rarely see them. They have their own special ways to stay alive in their frozen environment. For example, an arctic wolf's ears, snout, and legs are small to prevent heat loss. Its fur is white, which makes it hard to see in the snow. And an arctic wolf has two coats of fur. Its undercoat is thick, soft, and warm like a wool sweater. This fur keeps water from getting to the wolf's skin. Its overcoat is rough. This top layer of guard-hairs keeps a wolf warm and dry— water rolls right off of it.

An arctic wolf can sometimes go for weeks without finding food. It must be a top-notch hunter to survive. It can hear the slightest sound from under the snow, far away. It also has a keen sense of smell and sharp eyesight to help locate its prey (animals that are hunted for food).

Did You Know?

- The snowy owl is sometimes called the Tundra Ghost.
- A family of snowy owls can eat up to 1,500 lemmings in a few months.

Snowy Owls

Birds That Blend

Many birds fly south for the winter to escape the cold. But one of the largest owls in the world lives in the frozen north year round. Snowy owls keep warm with a dense layer of down (soft, fluffy feathers). They are covered with thick feathers—even on their legs and toes! Males are almost pure white. Females have white feathers with dark brown markings. Their coloring provides them with excellent camouflage. That means they blend in with their surroundings. Blending in makes it harder for predators to see snowy owls. It also makes it easier for the owls to sneak up on their prey.

Sharp eyesight, excellent hearing, and razor-sharp talons (claws) make these birds fierce hunters. And with necks that can turn around in nearly a complete circle, they can look in nearly any direction at any time!

Did You Know?

- Harp seals get their name from the harp-shaped marking on the back of adult seals.

- A pup drinks so much of its mother's fattening milk in its first 12 days of life that it nearly triples its weight.

Harp Seals

Pup Protecters

Harp seals live in the icy cold waters of the Arctic and north Atlantic oceans. They eat crabs, shrimp, and many different kinds of fish. Harp seals spend a lot of time on pack ice (ice not attached to land) that floats in the open ocean. They even give birth to their pups on pack ice. To survive out in the open, a baby seal has special ways to protect itself.

The most important protection is color. Adult harp seals are gray or black. But a pup is born with yellowish white fur. This yellow coat only lasts for two days. A mother does not leave her pup's side during this time. But when it turns a pure and fluffy white, a mother will leave to find food. A pup is often left alone for a long time. Its white fur provides excellent camouflage against the ice and snow. This makes it harder for predators (animals that hunt the pup for food) to see baby seals. Polar bears, sharks, and killer whales all prey on harp seals.

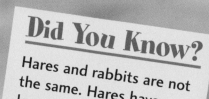

Did You Know?

Hares and rabbits are not the same. Hares have longer ears, longer legs, and bigger back feet than rabbits.

Snowshoe Hares

White in Winter

The snowshoe hare lives in Canada, Alaska, and parts of the United States. Bobcats, lynx, coyotes, foxes, hawks, owls, and eagles all hunt snowshoe hares. Because it has so many enemies, a snowshoe hare must be a wizard at escaping predators. Its main weapon is camouflage. Snowshoe hares can change color when their surroundings turn from the browns and greens of warm weather to the whites of winter. In the snow-covered north, many trees and shrubs lose their leaves in winter. When a snowshoe hare senses danger, it "freezes" and blends into the bare, white background.

A snowshoe hare's white coat is much heavier than its summer coat. This thick layer keeps hares warm in wintry weather. And both their front and back feet have thick fur padding. When a hare spreads out its toes, its fur creates a kind of "snowshoe" that helps it hop through soft snow.

Did You Know?

- To find enough food to eat, an arctic fox will travel more than 620 miles (1,000 kilometers) in one winter.

- An arctic fox's fur is warmer than any other mammal on Earth.

12

Arctic Foxes
Fast and Furriest

You can tell by its name that this fox lives throughout the Arctic. Like a snowshoe hare, an arctic fox changes color for the winter. It blends in with the grays and browns when its habitat is not covered with snow. By November, however, this fox has a thick, fluffy, waterproof coat. Its coat is so cozy that an arctic fox has no need to hibernate (sleep through the winter).

Artic foxes are low to the ground and have small, rounded ears to protect them from the cold. This fox will curl up in the snow and wrap its bushy tail around its nose and feet for warmth. Thick, furry footpads also help keep paws from slipping on the ice.

An arctic fox's camouflage makes it harder for its two main predators—human beings and polar bears—to find it.

Did You Know?

- Penguins have sharp barbs on their tongues that point in and help keep prey from escaping.

- Gentoo penguins dive into the depths of the sea to find food. A Gentoo penguin can slow down its heart rate from 100 beats per minute to 20 beats per minute during a dive.

- A Gentoo can swim up to 15 miles per hour.

Gentoo Penguins

Torpedos in Tuxedos

Gentoo penguins live in and around Antarctica. They spend much of their time in the icy water. Like other penguins, Gentoos are perfectly suited for swimming. Their wings, torpedo body shape, and webbed feet help them swim as well as any fish. A penguin's wings are much different from those of other kinds of birds. Most birds have long, flexible wings with wide feathers. A Gentoo penguin has short, stiff wings covered with short feathers. These wings work like flippers underwater.

A Gentoo penguin is dark on its back and white on its belly. This coloring helps camouflage it in the water. Predators from above have trouble spotting a penguin against the dark water. Enemies from below find it hard to see its white underside against the sunlit surface. A Gentoo also has special protection against the cold. Its dark topside soaks up heat from the sun.

Did You Know?

- Some polar bears that live in zoos have turned a greenish color. The color change was from algae growing in their hollow hairs.

- Polar bears are huge. They can be up to 11 feet tall (3.4 meters) and weigh up to 1,500 pounds (679 kilograms).

- A polar bear's blubber can be up to 4 inches (10 centimeters) thick.

Polar Bears

Arctic Kings

What kind of animal has fur that looks white but isn't really white? It's a polar bear. The hairs on a polar bear are actually clear. They reflect sunlight. Polar bears live in the Arctic—in the frigid waters and on top of the ice. A polar bear has many ways of surviving in the frozen north.

The clear hairs of a polar bear's coat are hollow. This waterproof coat allows a polar bear to shake itself dry and to remain free of ice. The hairs also trap air for added warmth and let sunlight through to the bear's black skin. Its black skin soaks up the sun's energy. Underneath its skin is a layer of blubber that stores this energy. Polar bears are so well protected from the cold that they often get too hot! To cool off, they rest or go for a swim!

Polar bears are excellent swimmers. They may look fat, but their blubber actually helps them float.

Did You Know?

A rock ptarmigan even develops winter feathers on its beak to keep it warm in the frigid north.

Rock Ptarmigans

Furry-Footed Fowl

When most birds sense danger they take to the air. But some birds prefer to stay on the ground. Birds like the rock ptarmigan must find other ways to protect themselves when a threat is near. Some birds have the ability to molt (shed their feathers). Then they grow new feathers. When a rock ptarmigan molts, it actually grows feathers to match the colors of the season. It has brown feathers in spring and summer. This allows it to blend in with the rocks and branches on the ground.

When snow falls, a rock ptarmigan grows white feathers. This makes the bird hard to see against the snowy ground. This way, it can hide from predators.

Did You Know?

- The Dall sheep was named after Alaskan explorer William H. Dall.
- The beautiful horns of the Dall sheep take about eight years to grow. They are made of keratin—the same material that makes up your fingernails.

Dall Sheep

Steep-Steppers

Dall sheep live in the mountains of Alaska and northwestern Canada. Bears, coyotes, and wolves are all a threat. These sheep have good eyesight and can smell danger from far away. A Dall sheep's hooves are perfectly suited for getting around in steep spots without slipping. Each hoof has a hard rim around the edge, a flexible middle, and a rough pad on the bottom for protection. The sheep even give birth to their lambs in these craggy spots. This helps keep their babies safe from predators.

Dalls are not very active during the cold weather. This helps them save energy. They have a thick, wooly under-coat and millions of hollow guard hairs. The hollow hairs trap air for warmth. They help protect the animal from icy winter blasts. Its white coat also helps the Dall sheep blend into its snowy background.

Did You Know?

A sheath is a casing that covers something. The sheathbill gets its name from the horny sheath seen at the top of its beak.

Snowy Sheathbills
Scrounging for Scraps

The American, or snowy, sheathbill lives near the South Pole, in Antarctica. It is about the same size as a pigeon. Like other birds that live in cold places, sheathbills have a layer of fat to help keep them warm. They also have cozy, waterproof, downy feathers. These white feathers help sheathbills blend in well with their snowy surroundings.

Unlike its seabird neighbor, the Gentoo penguin, the sheathbill is a land bird. This white bird stays along the shoreline. In fact, it is the only Antarctic bird that does not have webbed feet for swimming. The sheathbill must find all of its food on land. It must scavenge (eat leftover food or steal food) to survive. Not being able to fish makes living in the Antarctic even harder.

GLOSSARY

Blubber The fat under the skin of a manatee, whale, seal, or other marine mammal.

Camouflage Any behavior or appearance that helps disguise an animal in its environment.

Extinct When a plant or animal species has died out, and no longer exists.

Habitat The place and natural condition in which a plant or animal lives.

Migrate To travel when seasons change.

Molar A broad, flat tooth at the back of the mouth used for grinding food.

Species A group of similar animals.

FOR MORE INFORMATION

Books

Lynch, Wayne. *Penguins of the World.* Buffalo, NY: Firefly Books, 1997.

Lynch, Wayne. *Arctic Alphabet: Exploring the North from A to Z.* Buffalo, NY: Firefly Books, 1999.

Ovsyanikor, Nikita. *Polar Bears: Living With the White Bear.* Stillwater, MN: Voyageur Press, 1999.

Pielon, E.C. *A Naturalist's Guide to the Arctic.* Chicago, IL: University of Chicago Press, 1994.

Web Site

Learn more about arctic animals at: *http://tqjunior.thinkquest.org/3500/*

INDEX